In the Name of Allah, The All-Merciful,
The Kindest towards believers.

Disclaimer

All rights reserved. No part of this publication may be reproduced, stored in a retrieval system, or transmitted in any form or by any means, electronic, mechanical, photocopying, recording, or otherwise, without the prior written permission of the publisher, except in the case of brief quotations quoted in articles or reviews.

Contact: admin@islamiclessonsmadeeasy.com.au

Visit us:
Facebook.com/islamiclessonsmadeeasy
Youtube.com/islamiclessonsmadeeasy
Instagram.com/islamic_lessons_me
Islamiclessonsmadeeasy.com.au
Ilme.net.au

The pictures used are the property of Islamic Lessons Made Easy. The content and rulings are taken from various leading scholars and are presented in a simplified manner. Therefore, for the exact definition and explanation, please refer to the original sources.

First Edition
©Copyright 2025 Islamic Lessons Made Easy

Contents

Transliteration — 4

Introduction — 5

Etiquettes of Qurān — 6

Sūrah al-Fātiḥah — 8

Summary — 26

Glossary — 28

Transliteration

ا	a	ق	q
ب	b	ك	k
ت	t	ل	l
ث	th	م	m
ج	j	ن	n
ح	ḥ	ه	h
خ	kh	و	w
د	d	ي	y
ذ	dh	ئ / آ / ـا	ā
ر	r	ـِي	ī
ز	z	ـُو	ū
س	s		
ش	sh	ء	Read with a sudden pause of air.
ص	ṣ	ﷺ	Blessings of Allah be upon him and his family.
ض	ḍ	عليها السلام	Peace be upon her.
ط	ṭ	عليه السلام	Peace be upon him.
ظ	ẓ	ﷻ	Glorious and Exalted Is He.
ع	ʿ		
غ	gh		
ف	f		

Introduction

Tafsīr is an Arabic word that means 'explanation'; it helps us understand what the verses of the Qurān really mean. Scholars study the Qurān by looking at its language, the history behind the verses and other aspects. They also think about how the verses were revealed and how we can use these teachings in our daily lives.

Tafsīr helps us connect with our faith and learn how to use the lessons of the Qurān today. It makes the wisdom of the Qurān easier to understand and more useful for us.

When we made this *Tafsīr*, we worked hard to gather ideas from trusted scholars and important books. We wanted to explain the Qurān in a way that is easy for you to understand.

We hope this *Tafsīr* helps you on your journey to learn more about the Qurān and your faith.

Etiquettes of Qurān

Before reciting, it is recommended to say:
أَعُوذُ بِاللَّهِ مِنَ الشَّيْطَانِ الرَّجِيمِ
Aʿūdhu billāhi minash shayṭānir rajīm
I seek refuge with Allah from the accursed devil.

Then say:
بِسْمِ اللَّهِ الرَّحْمَٰنِ الرَّحِيمِ
Bismillāhir Raḥmānir Raḥīm
In the name of Allah, The Most Gracious, The Most Merciful.

- Make sure you have performed *Wuḍū* before touching any verse of the Qurān
- When reading the Qurān, it is better to face the *Qiblah*
- Make sure that the place where the Qurān is read is free from impurities
- Don't put the Qurān on the ground or anywhere it might get dirty
- Don't place anything on top of the Qurān
- When you recite the Qurān, try to pronounce the words correctly
- Take time to reflect on what the verses mean

After finishing your recitation, say:
صَدَقَ اللَّهُ العَلِيُّ العَظِيمُ
Ṣadaq Allāhul ʿAliyyul ʿAẓīm
Allah, the Sublime, the Great, has spoken the truth.

Sūrah al-Fātiḥah

Sūrah al-Fātiḥah

Sūrah al-Fātiḥah, also known as Sūrah al-Ḥamd, is the first chapter of the Qurān and holds a special place in Islam. It is often called the 'Mother of the Book' because it summarises the core teachings of the Qurān.

What makes this *Sūrah* unique is that it serves as a direct conversation between us and Allah ﷻ. It is filled with praise for Him and includes a request for guidance. Muslims recite it in every prayer, making it an essential part of daily worship.

The Holy Prophet ﷺ:

The reward for reciting Sūrah al-Fātiḥah is equivalent to reciting two-thirds of the Qurān and it is as though you have given voluntary charity to every believing Muslim, man and woman.

(*Majmaʿ al-Bayān*)

Sūrah al-Fātiḥah means The Opening. This name is fitting because it is the opening chapter of the Holy Qurān.

It also signifies something that opens or begins a subject, book, or even a connection. In this way, it serves as a key to open your heart to Allah ﷻ, expressing the deep love and devotion you have for Him.

بِسْمِ اللَّهِ الرَّحْمَٰنِ الرَّحِيمِ

Bismillāhir Raḥmānir Raḥīm

In the Name of Allah, The Most Gracious, The Most Merciful.

The word *raḥmān* means Allah ﷻ is the Most Caring towards everyone. *Raḥmān* comes from the root word *raḥm* (رَحْم), which also refers to a mother's womb. When a woman is pregnant, her womb provides everything the baby needs: food, warmth and protection. Even though the baby doesn't know or love the mother yet, she loves her baby deeply and cares for it without expecting anything in return.

Similarly, Allah ﷻ, as al-Raḥmān, takes care of all of us, even if we don't know Him or love Him back. Whether you are a Muslim or not, good or bad, human or animal, Allah's care extends to everything. He provides air to breathe, water to drink, food to eat, and everything else needed for life.

The word *raḥīm* also comes from *raḥm*, but it refers to Allah's special kindness and mercy reserved for believers.

الْحَمْدُ لِلَّهِ رَبِّ الْعَالَمِينَ

Alḥamdu lillāhi rabbil ʿālamīn

All praise belongs to Allah, Lord of all the worlds.

The word *rabb* (رَبّ) means someone who guides, nurtures, and looks after everything. Allah ﷺ makes sure that the stars, the moon, the sun, the planets, and everything else in the universe work perfectly together without any problems.

Isn't it right to thank and praise Allah ﷺ? He is the one who takes care of everything in the entire universe.

الرَّحْمَٰنِ الرَّحِيمِ

Ar-Raḥmānir Raḥīm

The Most Gracious, The Most Merciful.

Allah ﷻ repeats these two beautiful names here because they are very important. Al-Raḥmān reminds us of Allah's care and mercy for all creation, while al-Raḥīm highlights His special kindness to believers.

This also teaches us an important lesson: we should strive to be caring and kind to everyone—humans, animals, and even the environment.

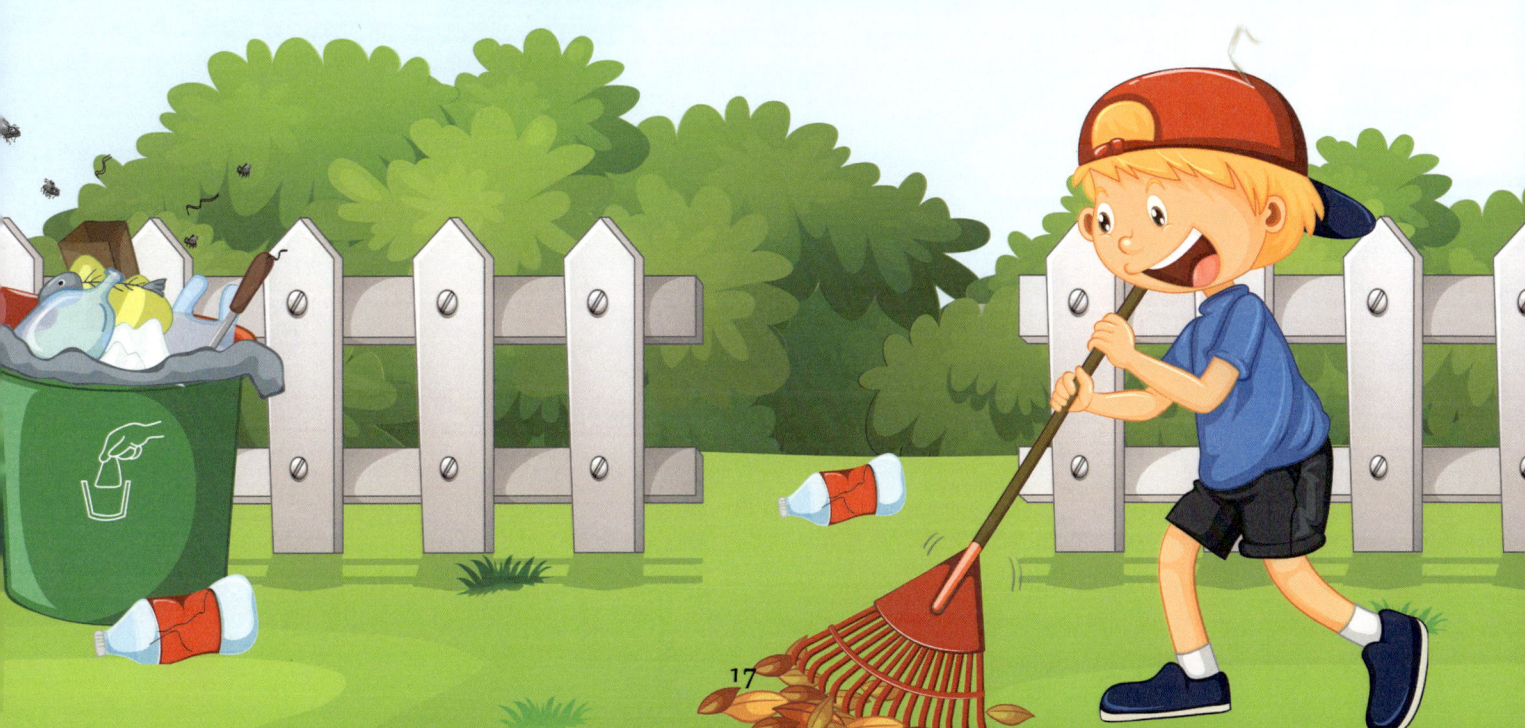

مَالِكِ يَوْمِ الدِّينِ

Māliki yawmid-dīn

The Owner of the Day of Judgement.

The word *mālik* means master, owner or ruler. It shows that Allah ﷻ has the ultimate authority and has full power over everything, especially on the Day of Judgement.

On this day, everyone will be held accountable for their actions, with good deeds rewarded and bad deeds punished unless forgiven by Allah ﷻ.

This verse reassures believers that Allah ﷻ is Just and that those who do good will be generously rewarded.

إِيَّاكَ نَعْبُدُ وَإِيَّاكَ نَسْتَعِينُ

Iyyāka naʿbudu wa iyyāka nastaʿīn

It is You we worship and You we ask for help.

This verse reminds us that only Allah ﷺ deserves to be worshipped and obeyed. It also teaches us that we need Allah's help in everything. Whether it's for guidance, strength or success, we depend on Him because He is the only one who can truly help us.

The verse says **"we worship"** and **"we ask for help"**, highlighting the importance of community. Worship and seeking Allah's help are acts that unite us as believers. It encourages us to support and guide each other to stay on the straight path.

اهْدِنَا الصِّرَاطَ الْمُسْتَقِيمَ

Ihdinaṣ-ṣirāṭal mustaqīm

Guide us to the right path.

Imagine your parents were driving a car and got lost. They wouldn't just keep driving without knowing where to go—they would stop to ask for help or use a map to find the right way.

In the same way, we ask Allah ﷻ to guide us to the right path. But what is this 'right path'? Is it a road we've never seen before? The next verse explains it!

صِرَاطَ الَّذِينَ أَنْعَمْتَ عَلَيْهِمْ
غَيْرِ الْمَغْضُوبِ عَلَيْهِمْ وَلَا الضَّالِّينَ

*Ṣirāṭal ladhīna anʿamta ʿalayhim
ghayril maghḍūbi ʿalayhim walaḍ-ḍāllīn*

The path of those You have blessed,
not of those who have earned Your anger,
nor those who have gone astray.

Here, we are asking Allah ﷻ to guide us to the way of people who earned His blessings. These are the Prophets, truthful ones and righteous people who lived their lives pleasing Allah ﷻ.

At the same time, we are asking Allah ﷻ to protect us from being like those who knowingly disobeyed Him and faced His anger, or those who strayed from the truth because they were careless or misguided.

Summary

Sūrah al-Fātiḥah begins with Allah's name, praising Him as the Most Caring, the Kindest, and the loving Master and Owner of everything. All praise belongs to Him.

Because of His greatness, we declare our worship of Him and seek His help. We then ask Allah ﷻ to guide us to the right path—the path of the Prophets, the Ahlul Bayt, and the righteous ones who earned His blessings.

At the same time, we ask Him to protect us from following the path of those who earned His anger or went astray.

Glossary

Ahlul-Bayt	- Family of the Prophet
Mālik	- Owner, Master
Rabb	- Nurturer
Raḥīm	- Specific care for believers
Raḥm	- Womb
Raḥmān	- Care for everything
Qiblah	- Direction of the Kaʿbah
Sūrah	- Chapter
Sūrah al-Fātiḥah	- The Opening Chapter
Sūrah al-Ḥamd	- The Praised Chapter

Credit

All praise belongs to Allah, the All Merciful towards all existents, the Kindest towards believers. He Who has given us enough patience and courage to complete this book.

Islamic Lessons Made Easy would like to thank all those involved in this project for their hard work and commitment.

CREATOR
Abbas Ibrahim

EDITORS
Kawthar Ibrahim
Sheikh Dr Zaid Alsalami

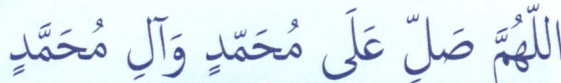

Allahumma ṣalli 'ala Muḥammadi(n)w wa āli Muḥammad
O Allah, (please do) bless Muḥammad and the Household of Muḥammad

Contact: admin@islamiclessonsmadeeasy.com.au

Visit us:
Facebook.com/islamiclessonsmadeeasy
Youtube.com/islamiclessonsmadeeasy
Instagram.com/islamic_lessons_me
Islamiclessonsmadeeasy.com.au
Ilme.net.au

www.ingramcontent.com/pod-product-compliance
Lightning Source LLC
Chambersburg PA
CBRC091202070526
44583CB00008B/182